ASTRONAUTS TODAY

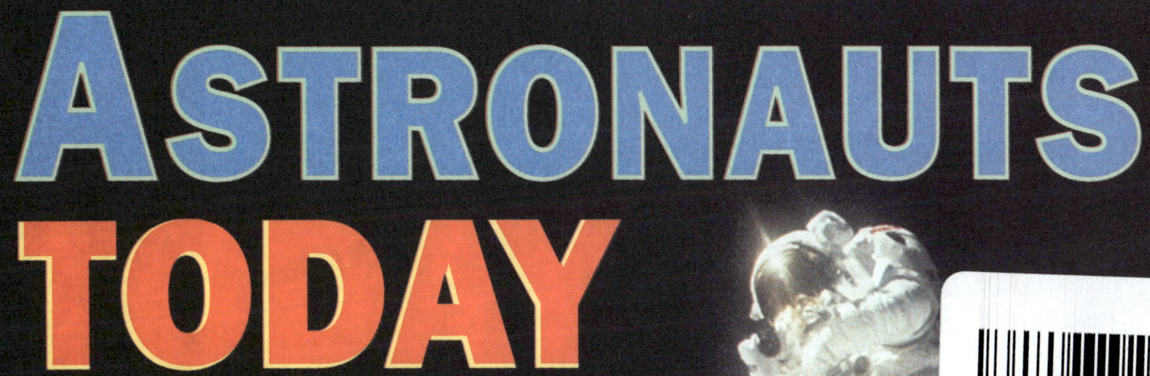

BY ROSANNA HANSEN

A Random House PICTUREBACK® Book

Random House New York

Published in the United States by Random House, Inc., New York, and simultaneously in Canada by Random House of Canada Limited, Toronto.
www.randomhouse.com/kids/
Library of Congress Catalog Card Number: 97-066888
ISBN 0-679-88194-8
Printed in the United States of America 10 9 8 7 6 5 4 3 2 1

The first astronaut ever to leave his spacecraft while in orbit was Edward H. White II in 1965.

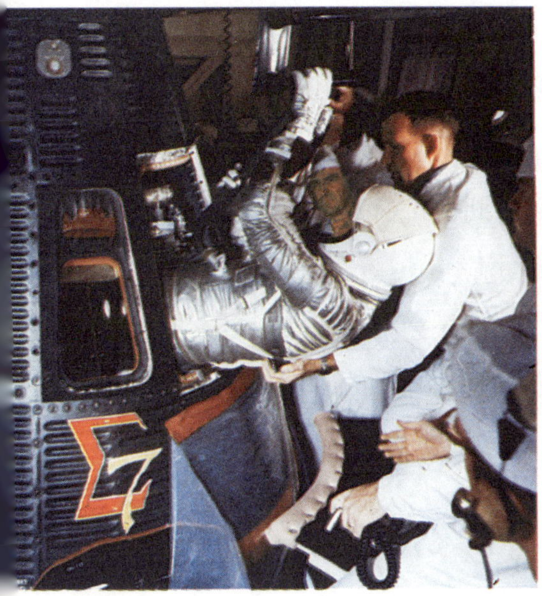

▲ *October 3, 1962: Astronaut Walter M. Schirra, Jr., climbs into a* Sigma 7 *spacecraft for mission Mercury Atlas 8.*

For centuries, people have dreamed of traveling into space. They have wondered what the moon was like. They have wondered if there is life on other planets.

In April 1961, this dream began to come true. Yuri Gagarin of the Soviet Union flew around Earth in *Vostok 1*. He was the first human to travel into space. In May 1961, Alan Shepard became the first American in space. After that, more Americans and Soviets flew into space. Their spacecraft got bigger and more powerful, and their flights got longer and more complicated. Spacecraft, spacesuits, and equipment were developed that made it possible to learn more and do more in space. Astronauts began training to use this new equipment and to prepare for all kinds of exciting journeys.

▶ *Yuri A. Gagarin, the first astronaut in space.*

▲ *Pilot Jon A. McBride experiences a few seconds of weightlessness aboard a NASA KC-135 aircraft.*

Astronauts must have special training. First, they must study very hard to learn about engineering, astronomy, and aviation. They learn to fly spacecraft using a simulator, or special model, that acts as if they were on a real space mission.

Astronauts also learn how it feels to be in space. On Earth, gravity pulls everything down to the ground. In space, everything becomes weightless. To experience this sense of weightlessness, astronauts go on special flights in jet airplanes. The planes drop in a free fall toward Earth, which causes all those aboard to feel as if gravity has let go of them—making them weightless—for about thirty seconds. It's a little like the feeling you get if you've ever ridden in an elevator that drops down quickly or on an amusement park ride that drops very fast from a height. So many astronauts get sick on these free-fall flights that they call the jet the "vomit comet."

Astronauts Frederick H. Hauck and Richard O. Covey get comfortable in the cockpit of a flight simulator.

Astronauts need to practice the jobs they will do in space. Pilot trainees spend months learning how to steer spacecraft to a safe landing. Other trainees, who are called mission specialists, practice science experiments or are taught how to operate a spacecraft's robotic arm. Some mission specialists learn how to spacewalk. They put on their heavy spacesuits and practice moving underwater in a big tank. Working underwater is the closest they can get to weightlessness on Earth.

Astronauts F. Story Musgrave and Jeffrey A. Hoffman work underwater in their spacesuits to practice making repairs on the Hubble Space Telescope.

Astronaut John W. Young of Apollo 16 *salutes the flag.*

In the 1960s, most astronauts spent their time training for a trip to the moon. On July 20, 1969, the crew of *Apollo 11*—Neil Armstrong, Edwin "Buzz" Aldrin, and Michael Collins—finally made that trip. Neil Armstrong was the very first person to set foot on Earth's nearest neighbor in space.

Neil Armstrong's footprint in lunar soil.

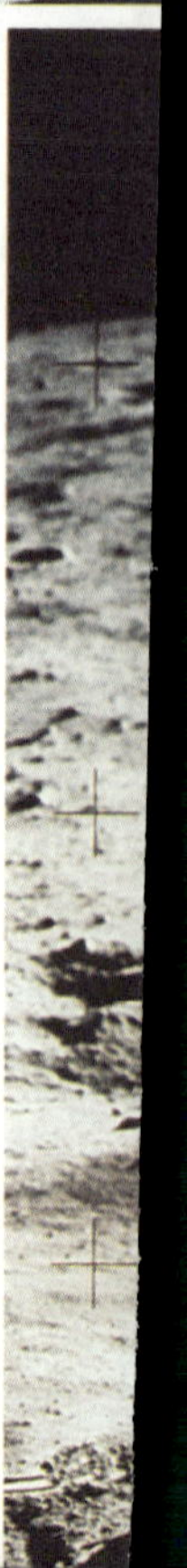

Together, Armstrong and Aldrin explored the moon's surface while Collins stayed in the command module, which orbited the moon. In their bulky spacesuits, the astronauts found that hopping was easier than walking. Because the moon's gravity is less than Earth's, it was easy to jump.

The moon is a strange, silent world. It has no air or water. It has no plants or animals—just rocks and dry gray-brown soil. The astronauts collected moon rocks and did experiments. When they returned to Earth, they were heroes.

Between 1969 and 1972, astronauts visited the moon five more times. No one has been back since then, but some scientists would like to build a space station there in the future.

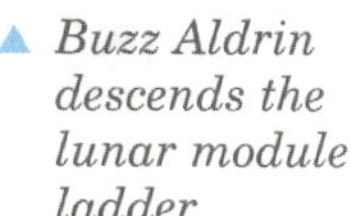

Buzz Aldrin descends the lunar module ladder.

Astronauts David Scott and Neil Armstrong remain seated inside their Gemini 8 *spacecraft after a splash landing. Welcome home! Years later, Apollo crews would return from the moon and splash down into the ocean too.*

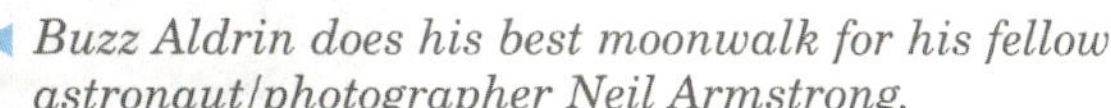

Buzz Aldrin does his best moonwalk for his fellow astronaut/photographer Neil Armstrong.

Since its first flight in 1981, the space shuttle has been our most important spacecraft. Like a giant delivery truck, the shuttle carries people and freight into space and back again, making as many as a hundred trips into space. Before the shuttle was developed, a spacecraft could be used only once.

The shuttle takes off like a rocket, with a fuel tank and two rocket boosters feeding its huge engines. After takeoff, the fuel tank and rocket boosters aren't needed and fall off the shuttle. Once the shuttle reaches space, it circles Earth in an orbit. Then the astronaut crew can launch satellites or do other work. Once the shuttle goes into orbit, everything becomes weightless. Clothes, food, books, and tools must be fastened down or they will float around the cabin.

The 100th U.S. human space launch is under way! Later, this shuttle will be the first to dock with a Russian space station.

▲ *It isn't all work being an astronaut! Astronauts Jeffrey A. Hoffman and Rhea Seddon still make time to play with a Slinky.*

◀ *Aboard the space shuttle* Challenger, *astronaut Sally K. Ride cleans out an air-filtering system.*

At first, being weightless makes some astronauts "space sick" for a day or two. But soon the strange feeling wears off, and the astronauts can have fun being weightless. They can float like a balloon and turn somersaults in the air! With no gravity to pull their bodies down, the astronauts grow one to two inches taller in space. They will go back to their regular height once they return to Earth.

To keep strong, the astronauts exercise every day. Without exercise, their bones, heart, and muscles would get very weak.

Astronauts can sleep standing up or lying down, but they have to remember to strap themselves into special sleeping bags so they don't float around the cabin!

There's always time for exercise! Even when you're in space, you can ride a bicycle ergometer—just like astronaut Catherine G. Coleman.

Most of the astronauts' food is cooked and then dehydrated before the space flight. This means that water is removed from the food in a special way to make it light and easy to store. Even strawberries and ice cream can be dehydrated! When it's mealtime on the shuttle, the astronauts add water into the food and mix it up. They can also heat their food in an oven. Some foods, like bread and candy, are the same as on Earth.

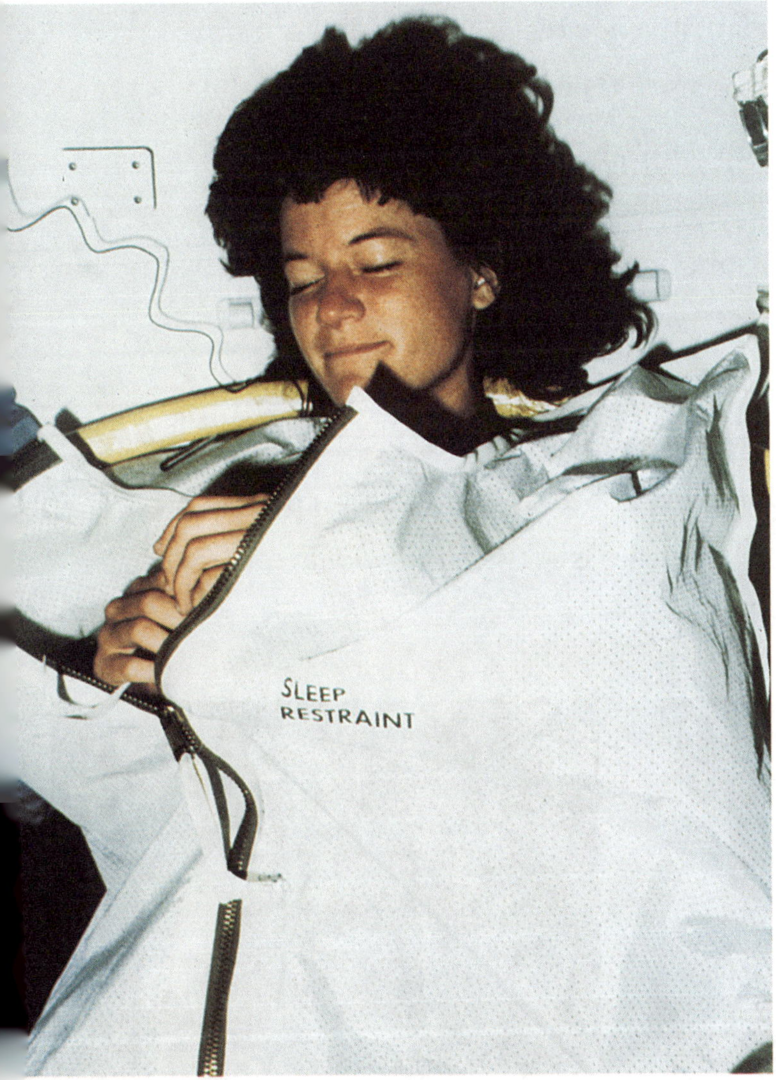

▲ *Astronaut Sally K. Ride uses a sleep restraint device to catch some z's.*

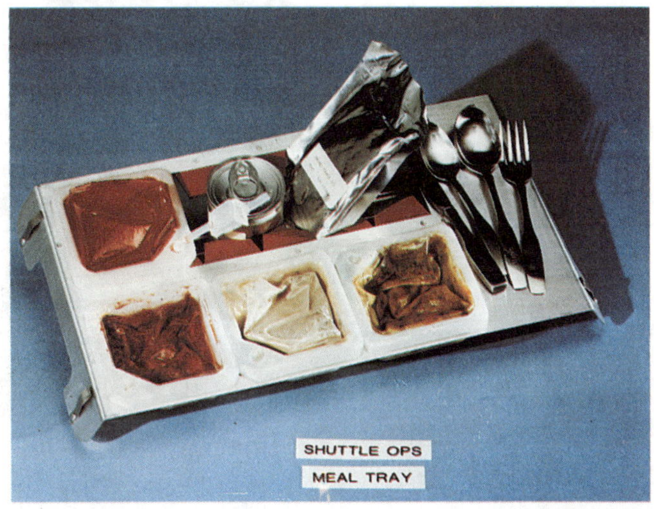

▶ *It's dinnertime. Tonight the astronauts will have cream of mushroom soup, smoked turkey, mixed vegetables, and strawberries.*

During a shuttle mission, astronauts have special jobs to do each day. Some work on science experiments. Others might launch a satellite or fix one that is broken. The pilot and commander steer the shuttle and fire special engines if they need to adjust their course. Some of the astronauts operate the shuttle's big robotic arm.

Some astronauts go out on spacewalks in order to do their work. To get ready, they put on long underwear filled with small plastic tubes. Water runs through the tubes and keeps the astronauts cool. Next comes the spacesuit—pants, top, helmet, and gloves. The astronauts are very careful when they put on their spacesuits. Their lives depend on the suits once they step into the huge, empty void of space.

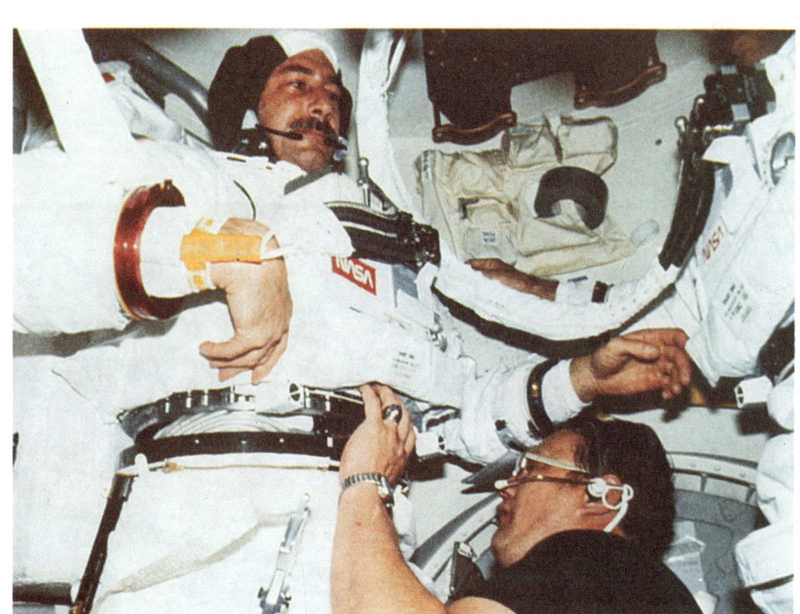

▲ *Mission commander Karol J. Bibko assists astronaut Jeffrey A. Hoffman with his spacesuit.*

▲ *Astronauts Jeffrey A. Hoffman and F. Story Musgrave make minor adjustments to the Hubble Space Telescope.*

Sometimes astronauts use a tool called a manned maneuvering unit (MMU). The MMU looks like an armchair, but this chair is jet-propelled! The astronaut makes it fly by firing jet thrusters. With an MMU, an astronaut can zoom away from the shuttle to capture a satellite and then bring it into the shuttle's cargo bay to be repaired.

▲ *With an MMU, this astronaut can go almost anywhere he pleases—within limits, that is!*

▶ *Astronaut Kathryn C. Thornton lifts the Corrective Space Telescope Axial Replacement (COSTAR). It is about to be installed on the Hubble Space Telescope.*

Planet Earth

When the crew is ready to come home, the pilot turns the shuttle back toward Earth. When the shuttle enters Earth's atmosphere again, it glows red-hot from rubbing against the air. Its surface is protected from burning up by special tiles that soak up the heat. The pilot lands the shuttle like a giant glider plane, without using the engines. It actually floats back to Earth!

The Endeavour *lands, bringing its crew home safely.*

Most of the time, space missions go smoothly. Sometimes, however, they are canceled because of bad weather or problems with equipment. And sometimes accidents happen, no matter how careful people are. On a cold January morning in 1986, the shuttle *Challenger* lifted off its launch pad with seven astronauts on board. At first, all systems looked good for a smooth flight. Then, after only seventy-three seconds, the *Challenger* suddenly exploded in a huge fireball of gas and flame. All seven crew members were killed.

After this terrible accident, all space flights were stopped while scientists looked for what had gone wrong. Eventually, they

▲ *The final crew of the space shuttle* Challenger:
(front row, left to right) Michael J. Smith, Francis R. Scobee, and Ronald E. McNair;
(back row) Ellison S. Onizuka, Sharon Christa McAuliffe, Gregory B. Jarvis, and Judith A. Resnik.

January 28, 1986: Moments after liftoff, the Challenger *explodes.*

found that the extremely cold weather before the launch had made the rubber rings in a small part of the shuttle too stiff and hard to do their job of sealing in hot gases. Because of this, the hot gases escaped and caused the terrible explosion. It took many months to find a way to fix the rings. Hundreds of other new safety features were also added to the shuttle to make it as safe as possible in the future.

Many times before the *Challenger* explosion, American astronauts had roared into space and returned safely. But space travel is not a simple, everyday event. When astronauts rocket into space, there is always a risk involved.

Sometimes people from other countries fly on the shuttle with American astronauts. And now other governments are building space shuttles of their own. The Russians have built a shuttle called *Buran,* which means "snowstorm." The space agencies in Japan and Europe are working on space shuttles, too.

Astronauts David M. Walker and Kenneth Cockrell are busy on the flight deck of the space shuttle Endeavour.

◀ *Mir, Russia's space station*

▲ *The space shuttle* Atlantis *as seen from* Mir *before docking.*

In 1995, American astronauts and Russian cosmonauts teamed up to be partners in space. Americans docked the shuttle *Atlantis* with the Russian space station *Mir*. Once they were joined together, *Atlantis* and *Mir* became the largest spacecraft ever to orbit Earth.

US.

During the *Mir* and *Atlantis* mission, the Russian and American crews quickly became friends. They did experiments, exchanged cargo, and went on spacewalks. They even found time to have a sing-along in space!

The linkup of *Mir* and *Atlantis* was the start of many shuttle visits to *Mir*. Sometimes astronauts would visit *Mir* for many months. During these stays, they did experiments and studied how their bodies changed during a long time in space. They also learned how to live and work with Russian cosmonauts.

◀ Mir *and* Atlantis *linked together, the largest space vehicle ever to orbit Earth.*

▶ *Astronaut Robert L. Gibson (in red), American mission commander, shakes hands with his Russian counterpart, cosmonaut Vladimir N. Dezhurov,* Mir *commander.*

Space stations like *Mir* are designed to be a home in space, where people can live for a long time. Inside *Mir,* there are living quarters with a bathroom area, places to sleep and to prepare food, and an exercise area. The flight deck has controls for flying the station. *Mir* also has a separate work area with telescopes and instruments for studying space.

▲ *Everyone joins in when cosmonaut Gennady Strekalov plays his guitar!*

The astronauts' visits to *Mir* are part of an exciting new project. Russians and Americans are working together to create a huge new space station! Building this international station is the toughest job people have ever attempted in space. The work will take many years and will require over forty shuttle trips. When it is ready, the new International Space Station (ISS) will replace *Mir*.

Building the ISS is taking lots of planning and hard work. That's why Russians and Americans are working together. People from Canada, Europe, and Japan are also helping to build the station.

▲ *Cosmonaut working to repair solar panels on* Mir.

With so many people working together, we can build an exciting future in space. When the ISS is finished, it can be used as a base for long space trips. The station can also be used as a scientific lab to help us probe the secrets of the universe.

Perhaps someday you will ride the shuttle to the ISS. At the station, you might operate a space telescope to help us learn about another solar system. Or perhaps you will use the station as a base for your trip to the moon or to Mars. And one day, many years from now, your children or grandchildren might even live on a space colony somewhere in a distant galaxy.

This picture was made by computer. It shows how the International Space Station may look.